Christine's Christmas Countdown

Christine Ida Harrington

Clink Street

London | New York

ISBN: 978-1-909477-34-6
Ebook: 978-1-909477-35-3

Christine is a retired hospital consultant.

Dedicated to my family.

Illustrations by Amy Valerio-Depledge.

Introduction

Every year, without fail during Christmas lunch, my father would say "always keep Christmas" and then he would thank my mother for making it so special. My other lasting memory is of my mother always taking great care to ensure that we all looked very smart in our best clothes at Christmas time. Because of these very happy memories of wonderful Christmases during my childhood I was determined to make Christmas special for my family.

It soon became apparent to me that as a busy working mother this was not easy. Every year I made lists which I kept and added to annually. After five or six years I had a fairly comprehensive list and found that organisation was becoming easier. My apparent lack of panic impressed my friends and family. I shared my checklists with a favoured few and they complimented me on my comprehensive coverage of the preparation for Christmas. Thirty years later I have now found time to share my lists with you.

Over the past thirty years there have been two innovations that make Christmas preparation a whole lot easier. Firstly, online shopping has dramatically reduced the time required for gift and essentials buying. Secondly, it is now very easy to lose weight safely and sensibly by following a regime that suits your lifestyle. It is important to feel and look good at Christmas.

Many of the "tips" arrived on my lists as a result of my omissions! Of course everyone's requirements for the festive season are different so this can only be a guide. Nonetheless, I hope you find this little book helpful and that you enjoy the preparation and the festivities of Christmas.

September

First thoughts of Christmas preparation should be in the **second and third weeks of September**. Make sure that you have a calendar prominently displayed in the kitchen or set up on your computer and get in the habit of looking at it every morning. Have a notebook or memo section on the computer for lists. Start now to make lists of jobs, presents, cards and invites, adding to them as ideas come to mind.

There are four things to decide now:

1. Are any renovations, decorations, repairs or alterations required in the home? Contact the appropriate craftsman now as many of us decide to smarten up the house for Christmas and workmen become very busy at this time of year.

2. Are you going to grow your own hyacinth bulbs so that they are in bloom for Christmas, looking lovely and smelling divine? You should! Buy some prepared hyacinth bulbs and bulb fibre and plant in attractive bowls. Once planted and watered leave in a cool dark place and check weekly for water requirements, keeping them just moist.

3. Do you want to lose weight before Christmas? It is important to feel good and confident in your appearance both as a hostess and as a guest. Also, you can enjoy the extra calorie intake which is inevitable over the Christmas period. You have twelve weeks before Christmas so if you lose just one pound a week you can be twelve pounds lighter and fit into your favourite clothes for all the Christmas functions. Research weight loss regimes to discover which is suitable for you. This can be confusing as we are now bombarded by so many recommendations about what is bad for us to eat. You may prefer to do your own calorie control—1000 to 1200 calories daily—with less than twenty grams of saturated fat intake daily and no added sugar. Study GDAs (guideline daily amounts) on food labelling so that you can work out your daily requirements and limits. If this is just all too much to cope with, eat from a smaller plate, reduce portion size and move your body more! You must try to increase your exercise. **Do it!**

4. Are you worried what your facial appearance will be like at Christmas, especially if you have lost weight? The solution is to start doing facial exercises now. You do not need to spend a fortune on topical preparations. We keep our limb and trunk muscles toned by exercising them so why not do the same for facial muscles? Open your eyes and mouth as wide as possible then screw them up tightly; smile as wide as you can then purse your lips; frown, then look surprised; raise and lower

your chin. In other words, grimace as much as you can, at least twenty times each session, as many times as possible every day. If possible, do it in front of a mirror so that you can have a laugh as well. Massaging facial skin using circular fingertip movements when you cleanse or moisturise will improve skin tone. Drink plenty of water to keep your skin well hydrated.

October

Check weekly: Your weight.

Your hyacinth bulbs. Keep them moist.

First week. Now is a good time to think about yourself. Start to consider what clothes you are going to wear for parties and over the Christmas period. We know which functions we regularly attend so now is a good time to list them and the appropriate outfits and accessories, bearing in mind you will be a dress size smaller. For each event do a check list:

Main outfit; accessories—shoes, handbag, tights, jewellery; makeup; nail varnish.

Remember practical clothing for the days that you are cooking and attractive aprons are a must, especially when the children are very young.

Make hair appointments now so that you have a choice of times to suit you and for the children if necessary.

Mid October. Start to think about a present list. Write a list and retrieve last year's. Jot down ideas as they come to mind. Remember: family, friends, work colleagues, child-minders, babysitters, children's teachers, helpers at home, gardener, etc.

If you are going to be cooking for Christmas during half-term make a list and shop for all the required ingredients for your recipes.

Last week of October. School children will be on half-term around this time and if you are working it is a good time to take a few days' leave. You can go shopping and listen to what the children say they would like for Christmas or ask Father Christmas for. If new clothes are needed for children's parties now is a good time, allowing for growth, to get them.

One of the most enjoyable activities at this time is to make the Christmas cake and puddings. Children love to be part of the stirring experience so check you have all the ingredients, implements and storage equipment.

Make time to:

1. Clear out a cupboard in which you can store and hide Christmas presents. Keeping them all in one place makes life easier later on.

2. Go through kitchen cupboards and pantry throwing out all out of date goods to make room for all the Christmas extras. Try to keep all the Christmas non-perishables together so you don't forget where they are and can easily locate them.

3. Do some gardening. It is very welcoming and indeed attractive to have colour by the entrance to your house when welcoming guests at Christmas. All tubs, pots and borders should be cleared of annuals and frost-sensitive plants. By your front

door plant up some tubs with winter flowering pansies and polyanthus. These are readily available from garden centres and low maintenance.

Event Checklist

Fuction: _____

Main Outfit: _____

_____

Accessories: _____

_____

Fuction: _____

Main Outfit: _____

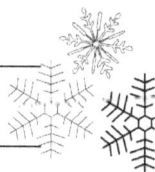

_____

Accessories: _____

_____

Fuction: _____

   Main Outfit: _____

   _____

   Accessories: _____

   _____

Fuction: _____

   Main Outfit: _____

   _____

   Accessories: _____

   _____

Fuction: _____

   Main Outfit: _____

   _____

   Accessories: _____

   _____

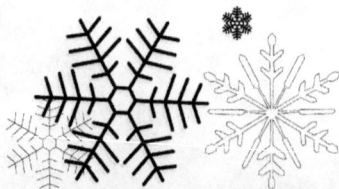

Dates to Remember

eg. parties, school functions,
hair appointments, orders, deliveries.

For you:

October: Function: _____ Date: _____

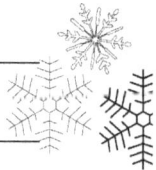

Function: _____ Date: _____

Function: _____ Date: _____

November: Function: _____ Date: _____

Function: _____ Date: _____

Function: _____ Date: _____

December: Function: _____ Date: _____

Function: _____ Date: _____

Function: _____ Date: _____

For the children:

October: Function: _____ Date: _____

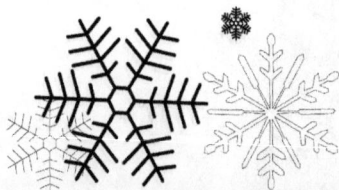

Function: _____ Date: _____

Function: _____ Date: _____

November: Function: _____ Date: _____

Function: _____ Date: _____

Function: _____ Date: _____

December: Function: _____ Date: _____

Function: _____ Date: _____

Function: _____ Date: _____

Presents to Buy

_____

_____

_____

_____

_____

_____

_____

_____

_____

_____

_____

_____

_____

_____

_____

_____

_____

_____

_____

_____

_____

_____

_____

_____

_____

Grocery List

_____

_____

_____

_____

_____

_____

_____

_____

_____

_____

_____

_____

_____

_____

_____

_____

_____

_____

_____

_____

_____

_____

_____

_____

November

- The weekly weight check should by now be very encouraging.
- Inspect cakes and puddings on a weekly basis, adding alcohol as desired.
- Sometime early in November the hyacinth bulbs will have produced leaves reaching three to four cm. Now is the time to bring them out of the cool dark place and to position them in half-light so that the leaves turn from yellow to green. Then place them in a light warm spot so that they grow rapidly and flower at Christmas. Water regularly to keep compost moist. If you would like more homegrown blooms at Christmas, plant an amaryllis bulb and some bulbs of the fragrant paper white narcissi now. Follow carefully the growing instructions.
- During this month party invitations will be arriving. Reply promptly, mark dates clearly on the calendar and arrange a babysitter if needed.

First week. If relevant, check dates of school plays and apply for time off work. Try to discover what costumes are required for the school productions and obtain details, material and sewing kit as soon as possible. Making angels the night before dress rehearsal is never satisfactory and very stressful!

If you are hoping to go to a pantomime and do not yet have the tickets you must get them now to avoid disappointment. Remember a babysitter if not all children are old enough to go.

Set the dates for parties and entertainments at your house. Send out invitations. Ask for response from decliners only but do request information about dietary requirements or allergies from attenders. Giving a reply-by date helps you keep a tally of the numbers and allows you to plan food and drink requirements well in advance. Cooking and/or buying to freeze early allows more time for last minute preparations. Remember that you may need a babysitter for your own functions.

Mid – End November. Now is the time to buy all the boring essentials that you will need over the Christmas period. Some goods you require irrespective of it being Christmas, some are regularly used items that you need more of and some are additions to the usual shop because it is Christmas.

Remember:

1. Cling film, kitchen foil and extra wide for the turkey, freezer bags, non-stick baking paper, ice cube bags, washing up liquid, washing powder, fabric conditioner, dishwasher tablets, cleaning agents, kitchen rolls, bin bags, toilet rolls, tissues, paper napkins, sellotape, light bulbs, firelighters, matches, toothpaste, toothbrushes, bars of soap, liquid hand soap, shampoo, hairspray, nail varnish

remover, tea, coffee (also decaffeinated), breakfast cereals, pet food, Elastoplast, Paracetamol, Calpol.

2. If you have babies, make a list of all their daily needs according to their age and get as much as possible now, in particular nappies. Have some thermometers to be on the safe side!

3. Discuss alcohol requirements and, according to taste, purchase wine, spirits, mixers, fruit juices, soft drinks, bottled water.

Special buys:

- Advent calenders for your own children and for presents.
- Wreath for the front door if you are buying an artificial one.
- Buy any additional decorations as desired while there is still a good selection in the shops.
- Christmas wrapping paper, brown paper and jiffy bags for posting parcels.
- Santa sacks and stocking fillers.
- Balloons.
- Christmas crackers, a must for the Christmas table to create a festive atmosphere, fun from the jokes and laughter from the hats. You can of course make your crackers. There are numerous websites with instructions.
- Music for Christmas. Check what you have for background music, parties and Christmas numbers. Now is a good time to review your collection, know where to find them and buy some new ones.
- Treat yourself to some good hand cream (so that

your hands don't portray how much work you have been doing!) and make sure you have very effective facial cleansing agents for removing the party makeup.

End of November.
- At this stage, try to get the number of guests that will be staying with you over the Christmas period. Request information regarding any special dietary requirements. There appears to be an increasing incidence of nut allergies and gluten intolerance. Research such problems on the internet well in advance if necessary.
- The guest rooms: Clean now, check all bed linen and make up beds. Ensure that you have adequate towels, soap, coat hangers and light bulbs and that bedside lamps and all radiators are functioning.
- Presents: Ideally Christmas present purchases should be nearing completion! If shopping time is limited spend an evening shopping online now.
- Check that Christmas tree lights are working. If old bulbs have blown, buy new L.E.D. lights which are safer and last year after year.
- Write cards. Spend a Saturday or Sunday afternoon getting the children to write their cards for relatives, friends and teachers. Try to get your own cards done now as this is a time consuming task. It may be easiest to do a certain number each day. If you are sending internet greeting cards you can leave those until later.

- The Sunday before the first Sunday of Advent has become known as "stir Sunday" as it is a popular and indeed appropriate time to do some cooking with the children.

Party Planning

_____

_____

_____

_____

_____

_____

_____

_____

_____

_____

_____

_____

_____

_____

_____

_____

_____

_____

_____

_____

_____

_____

_____

_____

Dietary Requirements

Guest: _____ Restriction: _____

_____

Guest: _____ Restriction: _____

_____

Guest: _____ Restriction: _____

_____

Guest: _____ Restriction: _____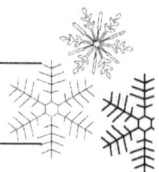

_____

Guest: _____ Restriction: _____

_____

_____

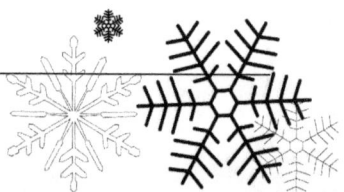

Shopping List

_____

_____

_____

_____

_____

_____

_____

_____

_____

_____

_____

Cards to Write

_____

_____

_____

_____

_____

_____

_____

_____

_____

_____

_____

_____

_____

_____

_____

_____

_____

_____

_____

_____

_____

_____

_____

_____

_____

December

You should be at least half a stone lighter now and bene-fitting from this. Perhaps time to treat yourself to a new outfit! Keep up with the facial exercises.

Early December.
- Keep checking the cakes and puddings. The first Sunday in Advent is another good time to get the children involved in any outstanding cooking that can be done at this stage. Check that you have ade-quate containers for storage of cakes and freezer goods. Remember that endless storage containers are required during and after the Christmas period.
- If you have to put in a butcher's meat order or a milk order do it as soon as they request it.
- Do you need to have the chimney swept? Many of us tend to use open fires more frequently around this time of year. I do know a family that had the fire brigade join them during Christmas lunch.
- A safety check before Christmas is a must if you have young children or are having them as guests. Place sharp kitchen knives out of reach. Ensure that accessible power points are blocked and that

no electrical devices or wires could be a danger. If elderly folk are coming, aim to minimise the risk of their tripping over rugs and toys.

- Hang a wreath on your front door. If you have not bought one you can make one using instructions from one of the many internet sites on the subject.

Household jobs.
- Clear, clean and tidy the fridge and freezer to make room for all the extra goods.
- Check all the glassware and any that is not in regular use should be washed and made to sparkle.
- Test your knives for carving and sharpen if necessary.
- Polish the silver and brass.
- Arrange to have the windows cleaned before Christmas.
- Inspect all table linen and launder cloths and napkins if necessary.
- If you don't have an attractive apron, do acquire one to protect your smart clothes when entertaining. A smart, perhaps amusing one for your husband or partner is a good idea, along with a chef's hat!

Other tasks to tackle now.
- If appropriate, make sure you have sufficient oil in the tank and order coal and wood.
- Buy your stamps and post overseas parcels and cards.
- Check children's clothes for parties and over Christmas.
- If applicable, i.e. your husband doesn't think about

his clothes until the last minute, find time to review them so that you are not sewing on buttons or pressing trousers at the last minute when you should be concentrating on yourself.

- Go through all your clothes and accessories and make any adjustments as required. Have them ready to slip into to avoid any last minute hitches.
- Remind elderly guests staying over Christmas to check that they have sufficient medications and to obtain a repeat prescription if necessary.
- If you don't have a hostess trolley, do consider purchasing one. This is a very useful appliance if you have a large number of people to feed.

Must do by end of second week.

Post all parcels and cards.

Write out lists of all the meals to be prepared and go through all the recipes. Remember to cater for meals for guests staying after the Christmas period. Make two lists of all that you require, one of items you can purchase now and one of fresh produce that you will get just before Christmas. Place internet orders appropriately or plan your shopping expeditions. You must allow for extra cooking ingredients and the fact that children will eat some of the goodies before Christmas. Therefore get plenty of olive oil, butter, milk, bread and cheese. Buy plenty of snacks and some special biscuits, not just for your organised entertaining, but for visitors who drop in unannounced. There is not always time to impress with homemade goodies.

You have hopefully completed the present shopping by now. Remember gifts for all your helpers at home and work colleagues. It is a good idea to have some unlabelled wrapped gifts under the Christmas tree to avoid embarrassment when the unexpected gift arrives for you or your family. Ideas for such lifesavers are: amaryllis bulbs, scented candles, soaps, potpourri, scented drawer liners, pens, notelets, bottles of wine. Buy some poinsettias, some for gifts and some to have around the house to create a festive atmosphere. Small variety packs are an option for children but they are often content to have chocolate money from the tree. While doing the final shopping lists go through all the games and presents requiring batteries and purchase adequate supplies of the appropriate sizes. You may also need additional adaptors.

Wrap any remaining presents. Children should deliver their cards to school and have presents wrapped ready for teachers on the last day of term.

End of second week onwards. If there are folk that you always visit, ring or email before Christmas, do it as soon as possible so such an important ritual is not rushed at the last minute.

Add some surprise for your regular guests by trying something new every year. The large German supermarkets offer a wonderful range of German and Italian Christmas food such as *Stollen* and *Panettone*.

The Christmas tree. This should be "installed" when you feel appropriate and the type you have depends on your preference. It is advisable to get one that doesn't drop needles too readily. Decorate it with the children. It may be slow but, along with opening presents on Christmas morning, it is one of the great joys of Christmas. If possible, especially when the children are young or you have pets, secure the tree by tying it with strong decorative ribbon or string to a window fixture. Check that all electrical devices and connections are safe and out of reach of youngsters. If time allows, do some homemade tree decorations with the children. This is a fun way of getting them involved and will give you lovely happy memories years later when you are decorating the tree by yourself.

Games. Christmas is a time for playing games. Plan them before the final rush. Check that all the parts—dice, etc.— are present in the favourites that you already have. Pass the parcel and charades are always a hit. Guessing competitions are easy fun and good time fillers. Of course you have to know the answers, e.g. the number of Christmas cards or the number of flowers in a vase.

I am going to detail one game that was a favourite for me, my children and now the grandchildren, mainly because it causes non-stop laughter and hilarity. Sit in a circle around a small low table. On the table have:

1. A parcel, with a prize in the middle and wrapped in ten layers of paper secured with loosely knotted string. In each layer have a prize (e.g. pens, pencils, sweets) or a forfeit (e.g. stand on one leg or sing until the next six is thrown on the dice).
2. Headgear, as comical as possible (e.g. a bowler, trilby, wig).
3. Gloves.
4. Scarf.
5. Spoon and fork (strong plastic if young children are playing).

The participants sitting around the table pass around a

tray with a dice in a suitable shaking container. Anyone who shakes a six must go to the table, dress up in the aforementioned attire and undo the string with the fork and spoon. Meanwhile the rest continue to pass the tray and shake the dice, with subsequent "six throwers" taking over at the table. It soon becomes a scene of great frivolity and merriment and certainly a source of memorable photographs.

Look at party game sites on the internet to get more ideas. Remember to have music ready for games that need it, and have prizes for the winners and sometimes runners up to avoid tears! Have some DVDs ready for children to watch during any bored moments.

Check that you have fuel in the car and a supply of de-icer.

Locate the snow shovel in case of bad weather and have some salt available for icy steps.

Now spend a little time on the home. Check that the plant tubs at the front entrance are looking attractive. Place your hyacinth bulbs in the hall so guests are greeted by their wonderful scent. If you haven't been successful with them, don't worry; buy some! Do get some fresh holly, mistletoe and evergreens to use as decorations around the house. They are so much more attractive and season-enhancing than artificial decorations. Christmas spice-fragranced candles, placed safely, produce a pleasant ambience. Even better, have mulled wine gently warming on the hob when expecting visitors. The smells associated with Christmas are welcoming and linger in our homes and memories. The aroma from baking mince pies and sausage rolls lets everyone know it is Christmas.

I always cook a ham on Christmas eve—another great traditional smell.

Two days before Christmas do find time to make some table decorations, preferably with fresh flowers and candles.

Water house plants as they will get forgotten over Christmas.

There are no hard and fast rules for the last few days running up to Christmas Day. Much depends on your plans, but do make lists and go through each meal very carefully at least twenty-four hours beforehand. That way you will remember to take things out of the freezer on time and can have food prepared for cooking. Write a time schedule for cooking so that everything is ready on time. In particular, be sure you know the time required to cook the turkey. Plan the table setting and do it the night before if possible. Make a list of everything you need to put on the table, from condiments to serving spoons. Select the wines so that they will be at the correct temperature. Remember drinks for children. Have babies' meals prepared well in advance.

So that you have as much free time as possible on Christmas morning, prepare as much as possible on Christmas Eve, e.g. stuffing, cranberry sauce and the vegetables.

For the Christmas pudding, have the holly to put on the top, the brandy to pour over it and matches to light it ready for a grand entrance with a flaming pudding.

You will now hopefully enjoy Christmas Day. Keep calm, feel good and forget your diet.

Meals to Prepare

_____

_____

_____

_____

_____

_____

_____

_____

_____

_____

To Purchase Early

_____

_____

_____

_____

_____

_____

_____

_____

_____

_____

_____

_____

_____

_____

_____

_____

_____

_____

_____

_____

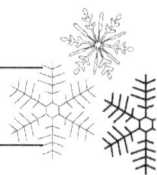

_____

_____

_____

_____

To Purchase Later

_____

_____

_____

_____

_____

_____

_____

_____

_____

Last-Minute Checklist

_____

_____

_____

_____

_____

_____

_____

_____

_____

_____

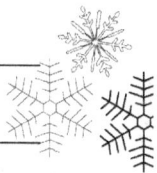

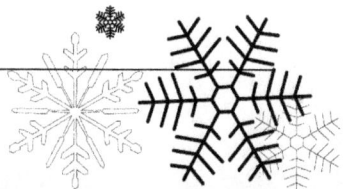

Cooking Schedule

Start time: _____ Item: _____

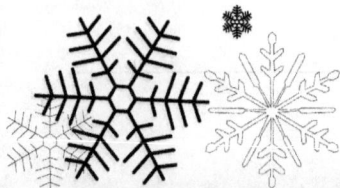

Start time: _____ Item: _____

Start time: _____ Item: _____

Start time: _____ Item: _____

Start time: _____ Item: _____

Start time: _____ Item: _____

Start time: _____ Item: _____

Start time: _____ Item: _____

Start time: _____ Item: _____

Start time: _____ Item: _____

Start time: _____ Item: _____

Start time: _____ Item: _____

Start time: _____ Item: _____

Start time: _____ Item: _____

Start time: _____ Item: _____

Start time: _____ Item: _____

Start time: _____ Item: _____

Start time: _____ Item: _____

Start time: _____ Item: _____

Start time: _____ Item: _____

Start time: _____ Item: _____

Start time: _____ Item: _____

Start time: _____ Item: _____

Start time: _____ Item: _____

Start time: _____ Item: _____